A Note to Parents

Eyewitness Readers is a compelling new program
for beginning readers, designed in conjunction with
leading literacy experts, including Dr. Linda Gambrell,
President of the National Reading Conference and past
board member of the International Reading Association.

Eyewitness has become the most trusted name in
illustrated books, and this new series combines the highly
visual *Eyewitness* approach with engaging, easy-to-read
stories. Each *Eyewitness Reader* is guaranteed to
capture a child's interest while developing his or her
reading skills, general knowledge, and love of reading.

The four levels of *Eyewitness Readers* are aimed
at different reading abilities, enabling you to choose
the books that are exactly right for your children:
Level 1, for **Preschool to Grade 1**
Level 2, for **Grades 1 to 3**
Level 3, for **Grades 2 and 3**
Level 4, for **Grades 2 to 4**

The "normal" age at which a child begins to read
can be anywhere from three to eight years old, so these
levels are intended only as a general guideline.

No matter which level you select, you can be sure
that you are helping your child learn to read,
then read to learn!

A DK PUBLISHING BOOK

Project Editor Shaila Awan
Art Editor Susan Calver
Senior Editor Linda Esposito
Senior Managing Art Editor Peter Bailey
US Editor Regina Kahney
Production Kate Oliver
Picture Researcher Martin Redfern
Natural History Consultant
Theresa Greenaway

Reading Consultant
Linda B. Gambrell, Ph.D.

First American Edition, 1998
2 4 6 8 10 9 7 5 3 1
Published in the United States by DK Publishing, Inc.
95 Madison Avenue, New York, New York 10016

Visit us on the World Wide Web at http://www.dk.com

Copyright © 1998 Dorling Kindersley Limited, London

Published in Great Britain by Dorling Kindersley Limited.

Eyewitness Readers™ is a trademark of
Dorling Kindersley Limited, London.

Library of Congress Cataloging-in-Publication Data
Dussling, Jennifer.
    Bugs! bugs! bugs! / Jennifer Dussling. -- First American ed.
        p.   cm. -- (Eyewitness readers. Level 2)
    Summary: Describes the hunting activities of various bugs,
including the praying mantis, wood ant, and dragonfly.
    ISBN 0-7894-3438-5 (pbk.) ISBN 0-7894-3762-7 (hc : alk. paper).
    1.Predatory insects--Juvenile literature. [1. Insects.]
I. Title. II. Series.
Q496.D87   1998
595.715'3--dc21
                                                                98-14975
                                                                    CIP
                                                                    AC

Color reproduction by Colourscan, Singapore
Printed and bound in Belgium by Proost

The publisher would like to thank the following for
their kind permission to reproduce their photographs:
Key: t=top, b=below, l=left, r=right, c=center

Biofotos: C. Andrew Henley 14–15; Bruce Coleman: Gerald Cubitt 24br;
M.P.L. Fogden 9bl; Peter Zabransky 17tr; FLPA: Larry West 23br;
NHPA: Stephen Dalton 12–13, 27tr; OSF: G.I. Bernard 29br;
J.A.L. Cooke 15tr; Planet Earth Pictures: Brian Kenney 26–27;
Warren Photographic: Kim Taylor 13cr.

Jacket: Telegraph Colour Library: J.P. Fruchet, front background image;
Natural History Museum: Colin Keates, front tl.

Additional photography by Jane Burton, Neil Fletcher, Frank Greenaway,
Colin Keates, Harry Taylor, Kim Taylor, Jerry Young

EYEWITNESS ◉ READERS

Level **2** GRADES 1-3

Bugs! Bugs! Bugs!

Written by Jennifer Dussling

DK

DK PUBLISHING, INC.

Stag beetle

Yikes!

Bugs look scary close up.

But <u>you</u> don't need to worry.

Dragonfly

Most bugs are a danger
only to other insects.
They are the bugs
that really bug
other bugs.

*Praying
mantis*

*Beetle-
hunting
wasp*

This praying mantis
sits perfectly still.
But if you are a bug,
watch out!
A fly lands on a branch
near a praying mantis.
The mantis fixes its
big eyes on the fly.

In a second,
the mantis lashes out.
Its front legs trap the fly.
They pull it to the mantis's mouth.
Munch, crunch –
soon the fly is gone!

Some bugs hunt other bugs,
not to eat themselves,
but to feed to their babies.
This hunting wasp
has just stung a beetle.

It will drag the beetle to its nest
and lay eggs on the beetle.
When the eggs hatch,
the young wasps, called grubs,
will eat the beetle up.

Hairy food
One kind of wasp
catches huge spiders
for its grubs.
It sometimes takes over
the spider's home, too!

Wood ants are tiny.
But they have sharp jaws
and they can squirt acid
from their bodies.
This acid can kill
another bug.

These wood ants
have found a dead bug.
Together the swarming ants
will tear the bug to pieces
and carry it back to their nest.

It is a quiet day by a pond.
One second, a mosquito
is buzzing along.
The next second,
a dragonfly swoops down
and snaps the mosquito
right out of the air!

Dragonflies are flying killers
that eat and eat and eat.
In half an hour, they can eat
their own body weight.
That's like you eating
250 hot dogs!

Ancient insect
Dragonflies were around
long before the dinosaurs!
This dragonfly rotted away
millions of years ago.
It left its print in a rock.

An assassin is a person who kills
another person on purpose.
The assassin bug is a bug
that really lives up
to its name.

Kissing bugs

Some assassin bugs
are called kissing bugs.
That's because
they often bite people
on the face.

When it catches another insect,
it injects the insect with poison.
The poison turns
the bug's insides to soup.
Then the assassin bug
sucks up the soup!

Only one bug
has to watch out for
a male stag beetle –
another male stag beetle!
What do they fight about?
Usually a female
stag beetle!

Short, sharp jaws

A female stag beetle
has smaller jaws
than a male.
But she can give
a much sharper bite.

The fighting beetles
poke at each other,
then lock jaws.

One beetle grabs
the other beetle
and throws him.
The loser
scurries away.

*Monarch
butterfly
caterpillar*

With so many killer bugs
and other hungry animals,
how do any insects survive?

Hoverfly

Click beetle

Some bugs have special ways
to trick their enemies.
Turn the page
and read all about them!

*Postman
butterfly
caterpillar*

Stinkbugs have glands
that make smells.
Some stinkbugs
ooze a nasty-smelling liquid
when they are in danger.
That's a big turnoff!

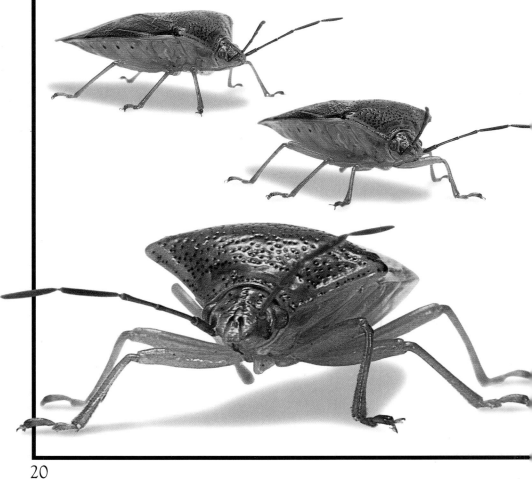

Stinkbugs are also known
as shield bugs.
Some use their flat bodies
to shield their young
from hungry insects and birds.

The monarch butterfly
looks easy to capture and eat.
But hungry bugs and birds
leave it alone.
Why?

In the insect world,
bright colors are a warning.
Bright orange signals that
this butterfly tastes bad.
Even the monarch caterpillars
taste awful.

Changing faces
When a caterpillar
is fully grown,
it changes into a butterfly
inside a hard case like this,
called a chrysalis (KRISS-uh-liss).

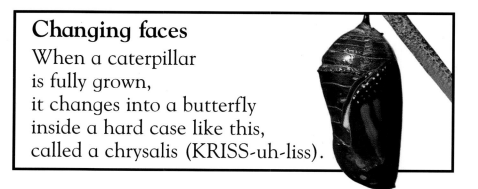

*Tropical lappet
moth caterpillar*

This caterpillar's long hairs
break easily.
When enemies try to catch it,
they get a mouthful
of hair instead!

Safety in numbers
Caterpillars sometimes
huddle together.
They flick their heads up
to startle a hungry enemy.

And this spiky caterpillar
can be deadly.
The leaves that it eats
make its body poisonous.
It is not harmed by the poison,
but its enemies are!

*Postman
butterfly
caterpillar*

A thorn bug is good at hiding.
It looks like a thorn on a twig.
A bird looking for a meal
might not see it.

Thorn bugs are smart, too.
They sometimes all face
the same way
and stay very still!

To avoid being eaten,
this click beetle
has a clever way of escaping.

It arches its back and then
jumps into the air.

If the beetle
lands upside-down,
it throws itself into the air again –
this time hoping to land safely
on its feet!

Flashing lights
Some click beetles
send out light signals.
These flashing lights
help the beetles
to find a mate.

One of these bugs
is a harmless hoverfly.
The other is a hornet
with a nasty sting.
Can you tell
which is which?
No?

Neither can most bugs and birds!
That's why they leave
both of these insects alone.
Still don't know which is which?
The fly is the bug
on the left!

Bug Facts

There are at least one million
different kinds of insects
in the world.

Sometimes all insects
are called "bugs."
But the true bugs are those
that have sharp,
strawlike tubes for feeding.

All insects have six legs,
and most have wings
at some time in their lives.

Some insects hear with their legs.
Other insects taste with their feet.

A few insects eat and eat
when they are young.
But when they get older,
they don't eat anything at all.

Some bugs have amazing vision
and can see colors
that people cannot see.

EYEWITNESS ◉ READERS

Level 1 *Beginning to Read*
A Day at Greenhill Farm
Truck Trouble
Tale of a Tadpole
Surprise Puppy!

Level 2 *Beginning to Read Alone*
Dinosaur Dinners
Fire Fighter!
Bugs! Bugs! Bugs!
Slinky, Scaly Snakes!

Level 3 *Reading Alone*
Spacebusters
Beastly Tales
Shark Attack!
Titanic

Level 4 *Proficient Readers*
Days of the Knights
Volcanoes
Secrets of the Mummies
Pirates!